Using Tools and Building a City in Minecraft

Adam Hellebuyck and **Michael Medvinsky**

CHERRY LAKE
Publishing

Published in the United States of America by Cherry Lake Publishing
Ann Arbor, Michigan
www.cherrylakepublishing.com

Reading Adviser: Marla Conn, MS, Ed, Literacy Specialist, Read-Ability, Inc.

Photo Credits: © Adam Hellebuyck and Michael Medvinsky/Cover, 1, 5, 11, 17, 21, 22; © Shadowman39/flickr, 7, 9, 23; © Classical Numismatic Group, Inc./Wikimedia, 13; © Oleg Troino/Shutterstock.com, 15; © Bananinha God/flickr, 16; © WONGIMAM/Shutterstock.com, 19; © Frédéric BISSON/flickr, 25; © National Archives Catalog/ARC ID. 196328/ Series: Franklin D. Roosevelt Library Public Domain Photographs, 1882 – 1962, 27; © AlesiaKan/Shutterstock.com, 29

Graphic Element Credits: © Ohn Mar/Shutterstock.com, back cover, multiple interior pages; © Dmitrieva Katerina/Shutterstock.com, back cover, multiple interior pages; © advent/Shutterstock.com, back cover, front cover, multiple interior pages; © Visual Generation/Shutterstock.com, multiple interior pages; © anfisa focusova/Shutterstock.com, front cover, multiple interior pages; © Babich Alexander/Shutterstock.com, back cover, front cover, multiple interior pages;

Library of Congress Cataloging-in-Publication Data

Names: Hellebuyck, Adam, author. | Medvinsky, Michael, author.
Title: Using tools and building a city in Minecraft: Technology / by Adam Hellebuyck and
    Michael Medvinsky.
Description: Ann Arbor : Cherry Lake Publishing, [2019] | Series: Minecraft
    and STEAM | Includes bibliographical references and index.
Identifiers: LCCN 2018035559| ISBN 9781534143135 (hardcover) | ISBN
    9781534140899 (pdf) | ISBN 9781534139695 (pbk.) | ISBN 9781534142091
    (hosted ebook)
Subjects: LCSH: Municipal engineering–Data processing–Juvenile literature.
    | Cities and towns–Computer simulation–Juvenile literature. | Minecraft
    (Game)–Juvenile literature.
Classification: LCC TD160 .H45 2019 | DDC 794.8/5–dc23
LC record available at https://lccn.loc.gov/2018035559

Printed in the United States of America
Corporate Graphics

Table of Contents

INTRODUCTION

You use technology every day. Many people do not realize how much technology is needed to design and build all the items we use in our daily lives. The fork or spoon you eat with, the transportation you take to school, and the shoes on your feet were all made using different technologies and **innovations**. Innovations arise when there are problems that need to be solved. Technology is also important for planning and building cities. Like in the real world, you will use different technologies to build your own *Minecraft* city.

Think about creating a *Minecraft* city. What would you build? What tools and resources would you need?

CHAPTER ONE

Tools: Building a City

You have probably used tools in your life to solve a problem. For example, if you need to write something down, you may use a pencil tool to do it. Tools play a huge role in *Minecraft*. You use them to chop down trees, dig in the ground, prepare the soil for planting, mine for materials, defend yourself, and create new buildings. In order to build a city, you have to use a wide range of tools.

Tools in both the real world and in *Minecraft* are made using different materials. In *Minecraft*, you may start building tools—like shovels, pickaxes, or swords—out of wood. These wooden tools are slow and break quickly. You can build stronger tools out of stone and even stronger ones out of gold and iron. But the strongest tools in *Minecraft* are made out of diamonds. The **properties** of these tools in *Minecraft* match those in the real world.

Gold ore is almost as hard to find as diamonds in *Minecraft*.

Most tools in the real world are made of some type of metal. Claw hammers, one of the most common household hammers, are typically made with specially treated steel and wood. But sometimes metal tools are not strong enough to do certain jobs. For instance, construction workers wouldn't use a gold saw to cut through wood or metal. In these cases, people use tools that are made of stronger materials like diamonds. Diamonds are commonly incorporated into machines and tools like cutting blades and drills. Diamonds are also used in dentistry, speakers, and computers!

You won't find many tools made completely out of diamonds in either the real world or in *Minecraft*. In *Minecraft*, diamonds are extremely rare and hard to find. This is also somewhat true

People have been using tools to solve problems since the beginning of time. Some of the first tools were made out of wood, stone, and obsidian, which were easier to sharpen. After about 2 million years, humans started using tools made out of soft metals, like copper. These early tools helped humans hunt larger animals. Later, when humans figured out how to pull iron out of rocks, they started using iron tools. These iron tools were much stronger than stone or copper tools.

Crafting

nothing (#0276)

+7 Attack Damag

When making tools, you have to be cautious of how many resources you are using.

in the real world. Diamonds are expensive in the real world, for the most part, because of how rare it is to find one in nature. In *Minecraft*, there isn't money. So, the value of an item like a diamond is measured by the difficulty of finding it. In the real world, diamonds can be artificially made through a special process using hot temperatures and extreme pressures. But in *Minecraft*, there is no way to create new diamonds.

People have to balance the cost of a tool with how strong they want it to be. People who build and use tools have to make a decision. Do they want strong tools that are expensive but last a long time? Or do they want cheaper tools that aren't as strong and need to be replaced more often? You may have experienced this same problem in *Minecraft*: how should you use the limited number of diamonds you have? Do you build diamond swords and armor? Do you build diamond pickaxes and shovels? You have to think about what makes the most sense when building your city.

When mining for diamonds, make sure to have an iron or diamond pickaxe.

SCIENCE

You may have built tools in *Minecraft* using gold bars. *Minecraft* tools made from gold bars are powerful but break quickly. The designers of *Minecraft* made gold tools like this to show how unique gold is as a metal. In the real world, gold tools may be pretty to look at, but they aren't useful. Gold is a soft and **malleable** metal. Any tool made out of gold in the real world, like a pickaxe, would quickly lose its sharpness and shape. Gold is a popular metal for other reasons. Unlike other metals, like copper or iron, gold does not tarnish or rust. This is because it does not react to elements like oxygen. Because of this, making jewelry out of gold became popular.

The best tools are made out of hard metals. But hard metals are difficult to mold into new shapes. Scientists have practiced combining metals with other metals or elements to create stronger metals. The resulting metal is called an **alloy**.

Gold has also been used as currency, or money, for over 2,700 years!

CHAPTER TWO

Cartography: Mapping Out the City

Now that you know about the tools used to build cities, you need to think about how you will organize the city in *Minecraft*. Have you ever wondered what your own community looks like from above? Have you ever tried to create a map of the community where you live? There are tools in the real world that can show you a **bird's-eye view** of where you live.

Satellite pictures give you a view of our planet from far above and show the distance between the continents and oceans. There are also cars that have 360-degree cameras attached to their roofs that take pictures. These pictures show different places up close. The satellite pictures combined with the street view pictures help us create a clearer visual of the world. Seeing the **architecture** of different areas from different angles, and seeing the way homes and shops are built, may give you an idea of how best to lay out your city.

Sketch out and plan what your *Minecraft* city will look like.

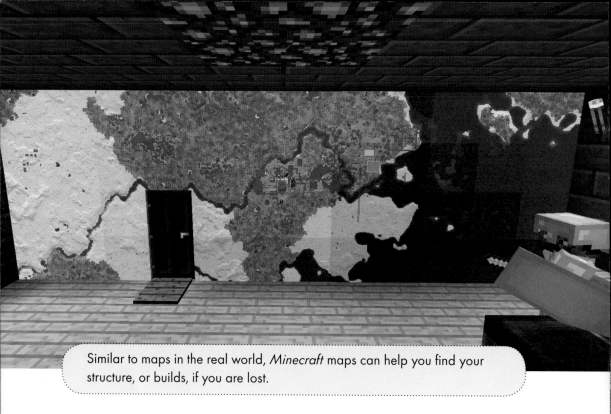

Similar to maps in the real world, *Minecraft* maps can help you find your structure, or builds, if you are lost.

Engineers use technologies like Google Earth to see communities from above. These maps can help them understand what certain buildings do and how they work together. People who make maps are called **cartographers**. There are many different reasons people use maps. Hikers use maps to stay on a trail. **Meteorologists** use maps to forecast the weather. City and urban planners use maps to determine where to put hospitals, fire stations, police stations, and parks. Have you thought about how the buildings and roads in your community work together? These questions can help you make decisions when you build your own city in *Minecraft*.

With an Elytra, you can softly land on the ground or water.

What if you want to get a bird's-eye view of where you'll build your *Minecraft* city? You can do this by finding and using the Elytra. The Elytra is a *Minecraft* technology you can wear on your back. It allows you to glide and fly through the air. The Elytra is rare technology only found in the End—the final dimension in the world of *Minecraft*. Once you have the Elytra, you can climb a high mountain, jump off, and soar through the air. This will let you see the ground below from a new point of view!

In the real world, designers have developed many technologies similar to the Elytra. Today's engineers are developing new ways for people to hover above ground and water. You may have even seen these on a lake or in the ocean. People have also designed drones to do many different jobs. Some fly high in the air to take pictures, while others carry people or other items over short distances. Engineers have also used magnets to make objects float in the air!

How will you get a view of where you want to build your community in *Minecraft*? Will you search for the Elytra? Will you find another way?

In *Minecraft* and in the real world, clay can be found in rivers and lakes. People have been using this earthy material for thousands of years to build homes and make pottery!

CHAPTER THREE

Material: Brick and Mortar

Now you have the tools to build your city and the ability to see it from the air. You need to think next about what type of material you'll use to build. While many people build structures using wood, the most sturdy and long-lasting structures are usually made out of bricks and stone.

Bricks are a great building material in *Minecraft*. Brick blocks in *Minecraft* are made by putting clay into a furnace— these blocks are among the strongest in the game. In the real world, the process of creating bricks is one of the earliest human technologies. Similar to the *Minecraft* world, bricks in the real world are created by heating clay at high temperatures. This process, called **firing**, changes the properties of the clay and makes it stronger.

Stone is also a great building tool in *Minecraft*. When stone is mined in the game, it turns into cobblestone. If you want to

Furnaces, like in real life and in *Minecraft*, can perform different tasks.

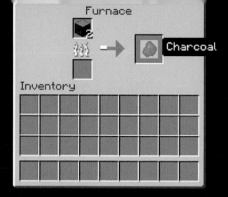

Furnace

Charcoal

Inventory

Try using resources such as coal to make torches.

turn cobblestone back to stone blocks, you must use a furnace. This process is similar in the real world. The only way to put pieces of stone back together to form one piece is to melt them using very high temperatures.

The furnace in *Minecraft* can change other objects into different material. For example, wood blocks can be changed into charcoal, which can be used to fuel the furnace. In the real world, charcoal can be used as fuel in place of regular wood. Charcoal burns hotter and longer than regular wood. People have been using charcoal as fuel for things like torches for thousands of years. In *Minecraft*, you can create a torch using charcoal and a stick. While torches do not burn out in

In *Minecraft*, TNT is made with sand and gunpowder.

Minecraft, a torch made out of charcoal in the real world would stay lit for a long time before eventually burning out.

Now that you know more about the properties of the materials used for building cities, what will you pick to make your own? Will you build it out of stone or cobblestone? Will you search for clay to heat into strong brick blocks? The possibilities are endless!

Using heat to change the properties of items is common in the history of technology. In the ancient Indus Valley, people wanted to build strong walls to defend themselves from attack. The people there didn't have a lot of stone, but they discovered they could turn weak clay into strong brick by heating it. Similarly, the Bantu people in Africa were among the first to figure out how to extract iron from rocks. They discovered that by heating up rock that had bits of iron in it, the iron could be separated from the rock and turned into strong tools.

Now that you have resources to build a *Minecraft* city, build on!

ENGINEERING

Another technology that people use when building is TNT. This technology was invented as a yellow dye and later was used as an explosive. Engineers and builders use explosives to blast holes in rocky areas, like mountains, that would otherwise take a long time to dig through. TNT is a unique explosive because it melts at a low temperature. This means it can be turned into a liquid and poured into containers. When it is a liquid, TNT is safer to handle and does not explode as easily. TNT also does not react to water, so it can explode in wet places!

TNT is similar to an explosive called dynamite. Dynamite is a **volatile** material. It explodes much more easily than TNT. However, if dynamite were combined with nitroglycerin, a chemical, it is more stable than TNT. Dynamite is used for mining and construction projects, like building road tunnels through mountains. TNT is used mostly by the military and in underwater projects.

TNT is an abbreviation for trinitrotoluene. It was invented by Joseph Wilbrand in 1863.

Extension Activity

In this book, we explored using technology to build a city in *Minecraft* and in the real world. There are many more different types of technology you can use in the game to make your city stand out.

One exciting piece of technology you can build is a fireworks launcher. When built, this technology will launch pieces of TNT into the air, where they will explode in a beautiful show. In order to make this launcher, you will need obsidian blocks, buckets full of water, dispensers, stacks of TNT, and a button.

Create a small base (two blocks high) out of the obsidian blocks, and place water in the bottom of the base. The obsidian and water prevent your launcher from being destroyed in the explosion. Place a dispenser at one end of the base, and place a button under it. Place another dispenser at the other end of your launcher, with a button under it. Load each of the dispensers with TNT. Then, push one of the buttons, wait a second, and push the other button. One TNT will explode and send the other TNT high in the air to explode!

Experiment with your launcher. What is the highest height you can launch TNT? What is the farthest distance you can launch it? What did you have to change to do these things?

What else can you build using the ideas from this book?

Find Out More

Books

Gregory, Josh. *Minecraft : Guide to Building*. Ann Arbor, MI: Cherry Lake Publishing, 2017.

Miller, John. *Unofficial Minecraft STEM Lab for Kids : Family-Friendly Projects for Exploring Concepts in Science, Technology, Engineering, and Math*. Beverly, MA: Quarry Books, 2018.

Websites

Smithsonian National Museum of Natural History

http://humanorigins.si.edu/human-characteristics/tools-food
Learn more about early humans and their use of tools.

Growing Synthetic Diamonds

http://viewpure.com/A4_l3pKhaJo?start=0&end=0
Watch and learn how scientists make diamonds using gases and why they need to create these diamonds for experiments.

Glossary

alloy (AL-oi) a substance composed of two or more metals, or of a metal and a nonmetal, fused together through high heat

architecture (AHR-kih-tek-chur) the designing and making of buildings

bird's-eye view (BURDZ-eye VYOO) seeing an object from high in the sky

cartographers (kahr-TAH-gruh-furz) mapmakers

firing (FIRE-ing) the process of drying or baking bricks in a furnace

innovations (in-uh-VAY-shuhnz) new ways of doing something

malleable (MAL-ee-uh-buhl) something easily changed without breaking

meteorologists (mee-tee-uh-RAH-luh-jists) scientists who study and predict the weather

properties (PRAH-pur-teez) important qualities of a thing

satellite (SAT-uh-lite) object that circles planets

volatile (VAH-luh-tuhl) something that can change without warning

Index

Adam Hellebuyck is the dean of Curriculum and Assessment at University Liggett School in Grosse Pointe Woods, Michigan. Follow him on social media at @adamhellebuyck

Michael Medvinsky is the dean of Pedagogy and Innovation at University Liggett School in Grosse Pointe Woods, Michigan. Follow him on social media at @mwmedvinsky